NORTH NORFOLK

WILDLIFE THROUGH THE SEASONS

James McCallum

© 1999 James McCallum
Arlequin Press
26 Broomfield Road
Chelmsford
Essex CM1 1SW

First Published as Limited Edition 1999
First Published as Limp Bound Edition 2002
ISBN 1 900159 81 3

Designed, edited and typeset by John Walters

NORTH NORFOLK

WILDLIFE THROUGH THE SEASONS

James McCallum

For my mother Diana

Hares.

A Barn Owl, having caught prey, shields it with its wings then quickly glances around before eating it. Wells Beach Road, March 1999.

Pinkfeet during a snow blizzard. A Richardson's goose from high arctic Canada was an unexpected find amongst this group.

Foreword

Encounters with wild animals and birds are memorable and exciting. They set the pulse racing and the adrenaline flowing. They are often unexpected and fleeting.

In response, an artist requires not only first-hand experience and a very quick eye, but artistic imagination and the courage to interpret what is seen in a personal way.

James McCallum has such a vision – one very much in tune with the modern passion for birdwatching. He is revealed, not as a restless twitching birder, but as a passionate watcher, letting events come to him; waiting with every nerve alert; witnessing moments of rare encounter that few humans see – the bittern and water rail; the pheasant displaying among indifferent hares; interactions between seals and terns; between flocks of waders, geese and gulls; groupings of such visual complexity as to confuse all the senses.

James does more than merely portray the scene, he reveals the intentions and tensions in every movement the animals make. His perceptive lines are full of humour and his colour conveys a delight in the light-filled landscape of Norfolk.

I warm towards paintings which make me say, "I wish I had seen that", (not only the event, but also the way it is painted), and this is my reaction on every page of this refreshing book. Had I actually been with James when he saw some of these events, I think we would both have fallen about with silent laughter.

This is wildlife art at its best. It points forward and opens new possibilities – a way out into fresh air. Take deep breaths!

John Busby

Stiffkey, looking northwards. July 1998.

Preface

North Norfolk is famous for its natural history. Its habitats are rich and varied yet have a quality of harmoniously merging into each other without breaking up the gentle undulating landscape or jarring the open horizon. It is a very subtle but, at times, overwhelmingly beautiful place. Many people find the subtlety too bleak and featureless, but for me it is a landscape of moods and feelings influenced by the effects of light, time, weather and seasons on broad open skies and vast tracts of delicately changing terrain.

When people talk of the wildlife of the area many automatically think of birds, in particular a few specialist species, or an almost endless list of rarities that have graced the area. Rightly so, but it is the wildlife within the local landscape that sums up north Norfolk for me: geese dominating the winter skyline; peewits on a freshly ploughed field; wood pigeons rising from farmland; barn owls hunting rough pastures; song thrushes shattering the dawn silence of a coastal village; rabbits and shelducks in sand dunes on early spring mornings with skylarks singing overhead; clouds of autumn thrushes and starlings finding the coast having crossed the North Sea; immigrations of summer insects or displaying hares and partridges livening up winter cereal. The list of combinations is endless and each day brings a different scenario.

When, however, I think of the north Norfolk landscape and wildlife I find it difficult to separate the human aspect from it. Familiar situations of worm diggers, fishermen, farm workers and local people going about their lives. Unfortunately these are changing times and this lifestyle of working and being part of the countryside and community that you were brought up in is increasingly threatened and fragmented. I greatly miss the community life of north Norfolk, its characters and folklore. This pattern is mirrored all over the British Isles and its effects irreversible. Fortunately the wildlife is still rich and hopefully the modern north Norfolk inhabitant will show it as much respect and affection as their predecessors have.

Finally, this book is not a guide to the area, in fact it is at times deliberately vague, being more concerned about giving a feel of the area through the seasons. The observation is from first-hand experience almost exclusively drawn and painted in the field. The writing and monthly introductions are summarised from fifteen years of my own bird and natural history notebooks and diaries.

James McCallum, Holkham, December 1998

Acknowledgments

Foremost I would like to thank my family, in particular my mother, for looking after and supporting me and for letting me do things my own way without interfering. To Andrew Bloomfield (the boy on the bicycle from the introduction) for his long friendship, companionship and valuable tip-offs as to possible drawing situations. To two Johns, John Walters (the friend I met in Cornwall) for his friendship, all the drawing days, constructive criticism and for helping me with the typing and design of this book. John Busby for his endless help and encouragement from the time I first wrote to him when I began drawing birds from life.

To all the other, friends and people who have helped or inspired me through ideas, advice, painting, writing or who have helped to colour my life in some way.

Lastly to Nigel Ede for giving me this opportunity to show my work in this way.

Mealy redpolls feeding on birch.

Introduction

North Norfolk is where I was born and where my immediate families on both sides originate. The area and its ways are what I know best and I am captivated by the natural history within its landscape. I feel strongly attached to the area and try to understand and enjoy it through painting and drawing its wildlife and landscapes. However, these interests have not always been a priority for me. As a child I was quiet and shy and content to stay within the confines of my family's home. My only outside passion at that time was a fascination in watching the lorries that unloaded cargo from the coasters at Wells Quay. As I grew older I developed a few interests but it was not until I was twelve that I found a subject that really enthused me. I can't remember one particular incident that started my interest in birds, it was a combination of things, but I enjoyed it immensely as it opened up a whole new world literally outside my front door.

I met a few like-minded people at school and teamed up with one of them. Armed with bicycles and some awful binoculars (how we ever saw anything through them is still a mystery) we spent out spare time discovering a new, exciting and often bewildering world.

My interest in drawing came later. I never really excelled at art in school, it was just an easier option than other subjects. Certainly the only wildlife drawings I made were time laboured pictures of the day's avian highlights. These were drawn from a combination of memory and copying from field guides, then placed in my log book the same evening. Like many school leavers I had no idea as to what I wanted to do.

I decided to go on to study 'A' levels at a nearby college but was going through a troublesome adolescent stage and my studying ended abruptly. The only way to salvage any form of education was to go onto an art foundation course. I really enjoyed this and found it refreshingly different from school. The disciplined nature of the course forced me to focus my energies and it became enjoyable to learn. There was a good working atmosphere in which anyone slacking felt excluded. We were being taught new ways of seeing, drawing and painting. I specialised in fine art and soon had another interest to compete with birds.

My interest in fine art was broad and thought based but I seldom combined it with wildlife until I moved to Cornwall to study for a fine art degree. I must admit that I didn't really enjoy much wildlife art at all then, but I did own four books that I really liked and inspired me. These were *Birds in Mallorca, The Living Birds of Eric Ennion* and *Drawing Birds* by John Busby and *Bright Wings of Summer* by David Measures.

I was introduced to another student when birdwatching near St Just in the far west of that county. We met up frequently after this and soon became friends. He owned the same books by John Busby and Eric Ennion and shared similar opinions about them. He was also equally inspired by the butterfly book by David Measures when he first saw it. We gave up our practice of 'working up' sketches of birds at home and began drawing them in the field, directly from life. This entailed intensive observation of the birds directly in front of us.

We were learning how to react to them by drawing so fast that the lines put down were what we saw and not what we thought they should be. It was a revelation and we became very critical of ourselves and each others work. It became a real discipline but looking back the drawings were awful. However bad the drawings were, the observations they contained were true and executed with honest conviction. It marked the beginning of a huge learning curve, the starting block to help free ourselves from some of the preconceptions we had developed towards wildlife art.

We broadened our horizons to other areas of natural history and began to teach ourselves to paint in the field. It was, and still is, a gradual process of continuous observation, making mistakes, then getting things right. Slowly we were becoming aware of some finer points of the behaviour of our subjects such as preening, scratching and stretching or how shadows and reflections joined the subjects to their chosen environments.

John Busby was a great encouragement to us and the following summer we participated in one of his annual drawing courses around the Firth of Forth. The course was a huge inspiration to all present. Towards the middle of the week we went to a high tide wader roost where we were encouraged to look at the birds as groups and concentrate on the sizes and behaviour of different species when seen together. This was a real turning point for me, it was the first time I had drawn these groupings and interactions between different species and it completely changed the way I viewed wildlife. It is still these behavioural and grouping situations of creatures within their chosen habitats which, when experienced outdoors, really excites me.

I made the decision to concentrate solely on natural history painting so decided to change my area of study to a wildlife illustration course in Wales. I soon became aware that this was a grave mistake for me. The emphasis on the course was more about finish and other people's requirements than about an individual's direct experience and interpretation of what they were seeing. I completed the course and returned home to Norfolk. I was happy to be back but felt dissatisfied with what I had received for my time spent studying.

I was encouraged to go on to further my education and apply for a place on a masters degree at the Royal College of Art. After a brief period working in local factories, to settle my debts and save for tuition fees, I decided to apply. I was accepted, the course was good and could be tailor-made for my requirements. The tuition was of a high standard and equally some of the students were of an extremely high calibre and I learnt much, if not more, by talking or working with them.

My time was split between painting in Norfolk, visiting college in London and working as a nature reserve warden in the holidays. The course also provided opportunities for drawing in other parts of the country and abroad. I graduated in 1996 and have returned to north Norfolk. I now divide my time between painting and drawing, seasonal wardening, conservation work and various part-time work. Although this can make living hard at times it does enable me to remove the commercial edge from my artwork leaving me free to pursue my own ideas. Some of the resulting images can be seen in this book.

A flock of barnacle geese amongst, brent, black-headed gulls and peewits.

January

January may well be the beginning of a new year for us, but in the natural history calendar of north Norfolk it is mid-winter and this month feels very much like an extension of December. The wildfowl remain in good numbers and there is often an increase in the numbers of white-fronted geese early in the month. In common with other wild geese these influxes later in the season often contain a good percentage of family groups, as pairs with young will remain on their breeding grounds longer than failed or non-breeding birds. The juvenile white-fronts lack the white foreheads and black belly bars of their parents, these features will gradually develop with age and moult.

The combined breeding and wintering range of our geese spans a huge area of the northern hemisphere. Therefore, it is not surprising to find a few individuals of other goose species which have lost their way on migration and joined up with our winter flocks at some stage of their journey. Bean geese from populations in the Scandinavian taiga or Russian tundra are scarce but regular additions, usually associating with large flocks of pinkfeet. Barnacle geese occur in small numbers every year and very occasionally in small flocks. Amongst our Siberian breeding dark-bellied brent geese it is not unusual to see one or two birds with light grey-buff flanks and bellies. These brents are of the pale-bellied race which breeds in Greenland and Svalbard. Rarer still is yet another race, with

a large contrasting pale edge to the rear flanks and a broader white neck-collar. This is the black brant whose breeding range extends from eastern Siberia through to Canada.

Most winters we are usually treated to a surprise visitor within the wild geese flocks. In past years there have been occasions when a beautiful red-breasted goose has joined the brents or a dainty lesser white-fronted goose has associated with its larger cousins. I remember well the surprise of my first snow goose with its white body and black wing-tips amongst a large 'V' formation of pinkfeet leaving a local roost site at dawn and the sight of my first greenland white-fronted goose feeding within the same vast flock of pinkfeet as two 'small' Canada geese from the far north of Canada. These sightings merely enhance the goose watching season, however, for me the predominant pleasure is to follow them through the season from arrival to departure, to watch their daily routines, the arrival of the first families, and observing the behaviour of the birds as they interact with the landscape. There is something primeval about wild geese, their travels and the way they fit into our seasons and countryside. Although they have to adapt and, in some ways, rely on how people manage the countryside, they still sum up the essence of true wildness and I can understand how geese and their movements became symbolic to many ancient cultures.

Waxwing

North Norfolk is famous for another type of goose, but this time an introduced species from tropical Africa which has surprisingly become naturalised here. It is the Egyptian goose, a resident of parkland where it nests high off the ground in large hollow trees, often favouring the hollow limbs of diseased beech trees. These birds nest early in the season and the noisy, elaborate displays of highly territorial pairs demand your attention. The disputing pairs display from either open parkland or high up in the nesting trees. In display they emit loud calls whilst the black and white wings are fully spread and the head points skyward. In the same areas woodpeckers start their drumming displays and the rich, clear notes of mistle thrushes compliment the scene.

Frequently a winter is made memorable by a species which appears in unexpected numbers. These irruptive species' appearances are often governed by food shortages within their usual winter ranges. Typical irruptive species include crossbill flocks searching for pine seeds, waxwings in hedges feeding on berries, fruit and rose-hips, jays after acorns, bramblings on beech mast or redpolls in birch woods. The redpolls acrobatics are great to watch as they hang from branches to reach the catkins. During these influx years several populations of the species can be brought together and it is possible to see the variation from the dark, nimble British birds to the paler greyer mealy redpolls from Scandinavia, through to the thick-set frosty white arctic redpolls often within the same birch canopy.

It is not just these smaller passerines that are forced to move outside their normal range. If small rodent populations are low in north-eastern Europe, large raptors such as rough-legged buzzards will be forced to expand their wintering range. The young birds, being less dominant, may be forced to wander further south. Several of these impressive birds may take up winter residence. They prefer farmland or the rough drier areas of marshes, with light woodland, in which to seek out rabbit warrens. They hover or hang in the wind above them like outsized Kestrels waiting for their prey to emerge from their burrows.

Bitterns

Bitterns are very rare resident breeders here. Although young birds from other breeding areas of Britain occasionally visit or settle here and immigrant birds from the Continent sometimes appear during freezing weather in the winter months at the moment there are only a couple of breeding females left in north Norfolk. With the lack of competition the male breeding with both these females has virtually abandoned his 'booming' song and the future of these mysterious birds here looks bleak. They are notoriously difficult to observe, especially with such low densities and huge feeding areas. I have seen them well on only a handful of occasions, usually as a result of pure chance but each occasion is memorable. I spend many winter days carefully looking along ditches choked with reeds or at freshwater springs during freezing weather in hope of a sighting but rarely with any luck.

One memorable encounter occured as I was cycling along the main coast road one warm spring afternoon, thrushes were singing from the copses and a loud chorus of toads was coming from the marshes. As I passed a length of roadside dyke I heard a rustle and looked down expecting to see a pheasant jump into flight. What I was looking at was a bit big for a pheasant then I saw the black moustache and staring eye of a bittern crouching just yards away. I almost fell off my bike! I pretended not to notice it and pulled up further along the dyke, then carefully worked my way back towards a nearby gate and began to sketch it. Obviously it had been taking advantage of the courting toads. Its objective now was to get out of eye shot. Like woodcock they rely on camouflage, not daring to move until you take your eye off them. Every time I looked down at my sketchbook for a split second then looked up again it legs had changed position. In this way it managed to move forward a few inches. After a while it became more relaxed in my presence and fed more freely. I was surprised to see it rapidly adopt its 'sky pointing' posture as a heron passed high overhead. Later it crossed an open field to get to another ditch network. It had done this by keeping as flat to the ground as possible with its neck fully stretched out in front. It then moved between clumps of dead thistles before disappearing from view.

On another occasion a friend informed me that a local man, while out walking his dog, came across a bittern standing in the middle of a field during a spell of frosty weather. We looked for it without success. A fortnight later I went down to the same meadows for a walk and stood next to an old fence covered with dead willowherb stems. The site overlooked a river-fed pool with dense sedge and rush choked edges. Having had a good look in and around the vegetation I turned to walk away and a bittern rose at my feet. It must have been standing tight against the nearest fence post. It gave an angry grunt as it flapped across to some nearby cover. I left it in peace and carried on with my walk. I looked over the same area several times over the next few weeks without catching a sight of it. However, a month later I struck lucky. Glancing down a short section of riverside vegetation I could make out patterning that looked like a bittern's back feathering. Then it moved and poked out a dark-capped head, with a beak shorter and blunter than a heron's, I was more than happy. This individual was great to watch as it moved along the length of river. To move forward it would push its head and neck under and through the vegetation then haul its back through the tunnel it had created, making a surprising amount of noise. After losing sight of it in an area of dense vegetation I moved in a wide arc around and down river of it, then slowly approached the same area by wading up river. Carefully looking through binoculars I searched all along the banks without success. Then, as I lowered my glasses, I got a real shock as I caught sight of its dark moustache literally feet away. We were both frozen to the spot, neither of us daring to move. I don't know who was the most surprised. With barely any detection of movement the bittern turned its head to face me, a sight so strange that it had to be seen to be believed. I carefully reached for my sketchbook and began to draw, at such close range I could even see its long eyelashes. Suddenly a rustle from the other bank and a water rail swam across the river, walked past the bittern and then ran off to some sedge beds where it was greeted by all manner of shrieks and squeals from other wintering water rails. Over the last few minutes the bittern had slowly sunk down onto its legs. It was now 'spring loaded' and ready for flight. This it did suddenly, without warning, sounding its usual grunt. I was left shell-shocked but overjoyed, standing in the middle of an icy river with a scrap of paper in my hand.

9

Drainage dykes with much emergent reed and aquatic plants are favourite feeding areas for bitterns.

Pinkfeet heading out to their night-time roost.

Pinkfeet landing on farmland.

Waxwings - Titchwell.

13

Woodcock feeding on open meadows at dusk.

Pinkfeet feeding on sugar beet tops. The central bird is a Russian bean goose.

15

February

February has an erratic, indecisive character. For one morning you wake up to a warm, still day of spring-like sunshine and bird song then the next you are back in the depths of mid-winter with ground frost, strong northerly winds accompanied by hail and snow. The songster who sang so vigorously and optimistically from the gable end of the house only yesterday has returned to being the local blackbird raking through leaves at the base of the garden hedge. These dramatic changes between the extremes of winter and spring weather may make it unclear as to which season we are in but it is so much more preferable to the depressing long periods of dull, grey, damp weather.

Despite this confusion and periodic set backs it is a short month and there is plenty to see and enjoy. Not only this but there are a few signs that we are progressing towards spring, albeit slowly. Grey herons have returned to their traditional heronries to inspect, repair and add to their large nests built from many year's worth of sticks and branches. Mistle thrushes are busy constructing their cup-shaped nests high up in an ivy covered treefork. Among the more traditional building materials the pair are incorporating long lengths of polythene and orange bailer twine. The drumming of woodpeckers is becoming more frequent and over the same trees at dusk woodcocks have begun their mysterious 'roding' flights.

In contrast to this activity the wintering white-fronted goose flock has increased in size. This will be the last influx of the season and in common with the other geese sexual displays and pair-bonding are becoming more evident and there is a great deal of antagonistic behaviour between the young birds.

It is a good time to head into the farmland, the winter cereal is still very short and allows good opportunities to watch the wildlife which inhabits them before it becomes hidden by the growing crop. Hares are performing well with males busy chasing females, interspersed with bouts of boxing. The game birds are beginning to display and become more territorial. Coveys of grey partridges, having been a close-knit unit all winter, begin to separate into pairs, the males often look great in the low, soft sunshine. The cock birds frequently stand bolt upright calling and showing off their chestnut brown, horseshoe-shaped belly patches. One will suddenly dart towards another pair resulting in a series of comical high-speed charges and chases. Cock pheasants have been fighting for some weeks now and, having established their dominance, the more successful individuals will be rewarded with many wives. It is great to watch a male trying to recruit potential mates to join his harem. To entice them he performs an elaborate display that shows off his colours and markings to their full extent. Slowly walking around a hen, tilting his body towards her and trailing his nearest wing on the ground. His long tail is fully fanned and also tilted, whilst the red wattles around his eyes are expanded and glow crimson red.

Back on the coast a few stonechats and the odd grey wagtail put in an appearance towards the month's end. These birds are moving back towards their breeding haunts in the upland areas of northern Britain. They have spent the winter in the milder climate of the south coast or on the other side of the English Channel. In the saltmarsh creeks rock pipits begin to show hints of the subtle slate-grey and pink tones of their summer dress. Towards the end of the month they too will begin to trickle back to their summer homes, this time on Scandinavian sea cliffs and beaches.

I watched this young great northern diver catching shorecrabs in the upper reaches of a harbour. By evening the tide had dropped so much that the diver was left to dive in a channel a foot deep. It became so confused and anxious that it began calling. This beautiful, eerie call I had heard as background noise for television programmes set in Canada and Alaska. I never expected to be hearing it ringing out on a still February evening from the Norfolk town in which I was born! After calling repeatedly between 30 and 40 times it took to the wing using its huge webbed feet to aid take-off as it ran along the surface of the water.

This white-beaked dolphin had washed ashore on an evening tide. It had recently died and was in immaculate condition, so I took the opportunity to make several drawings. As I was sketching a group of shorelark flew in to feed on the tideline.

A dispute between two families and a pair of white-fronted geese. These visual and audible displays serve to keep order within the flock without resorting to the extreme of violence.

Durham Wildm
14 Feb 78

roosting in pine plantation

A barn owl roosting in a dense pine plantation. Its presence given away by several dark pellets on the ground below.

The preferred hunting grounds of these lovely birds are the rough grass pastures, verges, dyke edges and field boundaries. This habitat has become rarer in recent years and as a result the owls suffer, particularly in late winter when rodent populations are at their lowest.

A male hen harrier
chasing a group of
shorelarks just prior to
roosting. This chase was
more for practice than
anything, nevertheless it
is always surprising to see
the harriers switching
from their leisurely
quartering flight to this
fast, strong, low-level
flying.

The seven shorelarks
arrived in November and
remained in the same tiny
area until the following
March. Their number
still intact, despite the
daily presence of
numerous raptors.

White-fronts dropping onto the freshes.

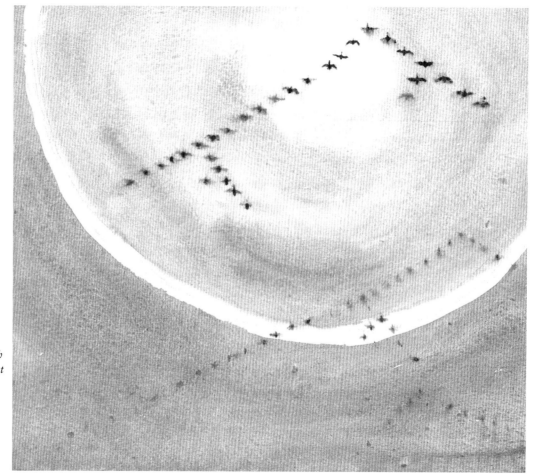

A bright but hazy full moon with skeins of pinkfeet passing in front of the moon and its halo. On moonlit nights pinkfeet, as do many birds, continue feeding. Their coming and going from feeding grounds and roost site continues throughout the night.

This very confiding penduline tit was a surprise visitor to the reedmace seed heads.

A threatening water rail chases a rival that has wandered into its winter feeding territory.

March

When one season ends and another begins is difficult to define. Winter does not finish on a certain day and spring begin the next. March, like September, is a month of distinct changes in the north Norfolk countryside. The bulk of the pinkfeet and whitefronts feel the pull of their breeding grounds. They are in peak condition at this time of year, having visibly put on fat reserves in anticipation of their long migrations and brief breeding seasons. One particular morning they feel the time is right and on leaving their roosts, instead of flighting to feeding areas, they begin their long return journies to their birthplaces. For several days prior to their departure they are often quite excitable and vocal. The pinkfeet are bound for Iceland, whilst the white-fronts head for Russia. They do not all travel together, some immature birds, or others that have not come into breeding condition, may stay for some while. The brents rarely leave before the end of the month, sometimes staying on into April. They breed much further east than the white-fronts and will eventually settle to breed on the Siberian tundra.

Redwings and fieldfares gather in large groups in parks and pastures near the coast. They feel the pull of their breeding grounds too, but will pause for a short while to feed up before venturing out across the North Sea. Unlike the geese these thrushes will depart at dusk for they choose to migrate at night. They must wait now for a high pressure system with clear, starlit skies and hopefully a light southerly air flow to guide them back to the Scandinavian woods and forests. I always have mixed feelings when the winter birds,

especially the geese depart. Initially I miss them, but it is great to imagine them moving north and to wonder how they behave on their breeding grounds. On the other hand I look forward with great anticipation for their return in the autumn. In much the same way I wonder about the places and situations our summer visitors have been experiencing during their 'winter' and long migrations.

One of the first back are chiffchaffs. It is great to see and hear them. Singing from sprays of sallow blossom, on the first warm spring mornings alongside bumblebees and brimstone butterflies just out of hibernation. Other summer migrants have arrived too. Wheatears, stonechats, black redstarts and ring ouzels pass through the dunes and horse paddocks on their way to northern moorlands. Last autumn's immigrant goldcrests make their return journeys in small groups through scrub and coastal pines.

Occasional firecrests appear in the brambles at this time. These two crests are the smallest of Britain's birds, barely over three inches long. Although they pass through on their migrations each year, I still find it difficult to grasp that these tiny birds are genetically programmed to set out across a vast area of open sea at night. Then on reaching land to make their way to some remote area of forest to breed and then return along the same route the following autumn. It seems even more peculiar that in the very same pines in which these goldcrests are passing are other

Black Redstart

26

individuals of the same species that are totally sedentary and will never leave one small area.

Over fields and marshes large, loose flocks of meadow pipits pass westwards and the first sand martins flash by. Many of these birds are still heading northwards and soon move through only to be replaced by a fresh wave of arrivals. Some migrants, such as Sandwich terns, avocets and marsh harriers, may well have completed the last leg of their journeys and will remain to breed. Indeed, some male marsh harriers often begin building on arrival. Looking closer at their markings you can often recognise the same individuals from the previous season.

Some of these large raptors have prior knowledge of the most suitable nesting areas, so, for them, it is a simple matter of tidying up and adding new material to nesting platforms in the reedbeds. The bases of these platforms may well have been started over a decade ago by some distant relation.

A pair of tawny owls roost high up in a cedar tree. A treecreeper, concentrating on its methodical search for food, appears oblivious to their presence.

6 March 1997

The first real warm, sunny spring day of the year and a distinct jump from winter to spring. After a rainy end to the previous day, this one started off with a clear starlit sky, perfect for a day's excursion to the Breckland heaths and forests. As I left the house just prior to dawn, I was immediately aware of the the absolute silence. Looking into the north-east corner of the sky was a most stunning vision, the now famous Hale-Bopp comet that had recently appeared in the media. The glowing head with its vast vapour trail was so dramatic that the carefully drawn out constellation charts plotting its position were quite unnecessary for locating it. A good omen indeed for today's trip which was a great success. However, it was not this excursion but the subtle and quite profound changes the warm sun made to the coastal marshes, when we returned that afternoon, which made the day.

Peewits, having broken away from their large winter flocks moved to some of their traditional nesting areas and the cocks were performing their dramatic display flights. The farmland close to the coast rang out with calls and displays of two other waders, ringed plovers and oystercatchers. Although the large herring gulls had been on territory for some time now, the saltmarsh at Wells was suddenly white with the arrival of the black-headed gull colony. The combination of several thousand of their calls produced a constant noise complementary to the natural sounds of the shore. Having paid close, even almost obsessive, attention to the wild geese over the last few weeks, my only regret in having left the coast for this day was, as it soon became apparent, a large proportion of pinkfeet had departed, presumably on leaving the roost that morning. Their departure was reflected by a steady stream of meadow pipits gently making their way westwards through fields and meadows. Avocets too had felt the urge to return to breeding haunts and many small parties could be seen and heard commuting from the fresh marshes to salty creeks.

Brimstones had come out from hibernation in force and were joined by lesser numbers of commas and the odd tatty peacock butterfly. The warmth of sun provided extra stimulus to the frogs, that had recently returned to the ditches and small pools, as frog spawn appeared in abundance. The following day was dull and cold with a freshening south-west wind plunging some of the action back into mid-winter, however some of these changes were irreversible and were a rung up the ladder to springtime which was echoed all around the countryside. I listened for the dawn chorus the next day which was distinctly fuller and louder.

Bird behaviour makes for fascinating study and is often quite dramatic. This dispute between nuthatches was no exception.

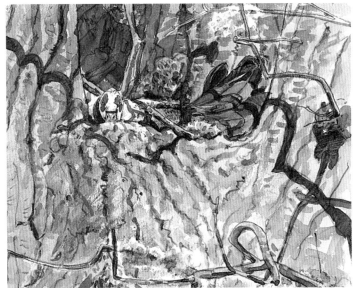

An Egyptian goose nests high up in a hollow oak bough. Initially all that could be seen of her was her eyes peeping through a thick ball of down. As soon as the young have all hatched they will jump from this hollow and the parents quickly escort them to the safety of open water.

I just missed the young leave this hole. As I arrived one day the mother had gathered her young in a tight ball behind her then the pair took them to a nearby lake. Vast clouds of down covered the trees and ground in the vicinity of the nest site.

The spectacular and complex courtship displays of goldeneyes.

March 16   bright
cold

April

The first swallow of the year traditionally symbolises the fact that spring is upon us. To older generations, who were brought up with more direct contact and stronger ties with the countryside, the first swallow of the year was a cause for celebration and a topical news item. Swallows can occasionally be seen here in March but in most years they are first encountered in early April. In my early birdwatching days regular evening visits to Holkham Lake would usually provide an early record as open water provides reliable feeding for them and thick vegetation, such as reedbeds, provide them with a good roost site. Nowadays I purposefully avoid such routines, enjoying the surprise element of the sight and situation of my first-returning swallow.

The momentum of migration picks up daily and warm, sunny days with southerly winds often result in a big flush of summer birds. Hot on the heels of the swallow are house martins, mixed flocks of these and swallows pause briefly in sheltered locations where airborne insects swarm. The rich, fluty song of a blackcap flows from the deciduous understorey and among the increasing numbers of chiffchaffs the first willow warbers begin to appear. Although appearing quite similar their songs are very different. The chiffchaff's song is a pleasant repetition of its own name, whereas the willow warbler has, in my opinion, one of the most beautiful songs of all British birds. Starting with a high, loud note it descends the scale, decreasing in volume but increasing in speed and ending with a flourish of notes.

Another new arrival is the grasshoppper warbler. These birds are named after their song, which sounds similar to a colony of bush-crickets. They prefer rank meadows with scrub, a habitat that is not common or, for that matter, encouraged even within some of the larger coastal nature reserves, so they remain scarce breeders. The sedge warbler on the other hand fares well as it prefers marshy areas dotted with bushes. Its loud, chattering song is interwoven with much mimicry of other species. When the first females arrive the males' singing becomes more vigorous and is combined with short, fluttering song-flights. The closely related reed warbler is well named as it favours stands of reeds. The first individuals are usually heard singing from this habitat towards the end of the month. It is also a favourite host species for the parasitic cuckoo. Having arrived a week or two earlier some cuckoos eagerly await this warbler's appearance, whilst others keep a close eye on the progress of the dunnocks breeding activity in the neighbouring scrub.

Peewit chicks

A newly arrived whitethroat gives a few scratchy snaps of song between bouts of feeding from inside dense bramble cover, whilst overhead migrating yellow wagtails and tree pipits emit their flights calls.

On the seashore little and common terns are back in residence, hovering and diving for whitebait and sand-eels. Some pairs are performing dramatic courtship flights at high altitude and speed, while others are involved in elaborate ceremonies on the sands.

In the gardens and copses, of towns and villages, blackbirds and song thrushes are busy feeding youngsters, some of which have already fledged. Their parents are extremely anxious for the welfare of the fledglings amid the large cat populations in these areas. Other young birds are also to be seen, mallards, coots and moorhens with tiny young feed in the waterways. On the grazing marshes are several families of peewits, the young birds, although tiny and covered in down, echo many of the characteristic stances of the adults. Many of these waders are at different stages of nesting, while others are performing display flights. They are now joined by several other species, all with very different aerial performances. Redshanks ascend singing with fluttering 'butterfly' wing-actions. After reaching the climax of the display they descend almost to the ground before repeating the action. This will be performed several times before the male lands holding his outstretched wings vertically behind his back for a couple of seconds before closing them. Higher still is a curious and wonderful display. A snipe flies high over his territory, suddenly gliding vertically downwards with neck outstretched, his wings open and tail fanned. As he begins to descend he forces his two outermost tail feathers to point at almost 90° to his body. The air flow over these feathers causes them to vibrate and produce a peculiar loud noise known as 'drumming'. Then as suddenly as he began to dive he pulls out and mounts the air again. This drumming display is usually repeated soon afterwards as he marks out the boundary of his territory. A female flies up and is pursued by another male, the drumming bird joins the chase too. One of the males glides above her with wings outstretched and held in a 'v' above his back. Suddenly he flips upside down and glides for a few seconds in this position before continuing the chase. Higher still are the faint shrieks of a male marsh harrier. He can just be seen as a tiny dot performing deep, steep undulating dives. Without warning he dives downwards in tumbling spirals, appearing to be out of control, while calling frantically. Then with legs and feet fully outstretched and wings and tail braking the airflow he heads for the centre of a reedbed. Then the female flies up calling and, as the male is stalling above her, she flips over and they disappear into the reeds with their talons clasped together.

Shelduck and black-headed gulls on a fine spring evening.

The dramatic courtship display of the male marsh harrier is often missed as it is performed at such a high altitude. The accompanying call of the male is the best way of pinpointing this display flight. Once learnt it is surprising how often you see it. I have even seen it performed high over coastal towns during shopping trips!

37

Hares

Fortunately these beautifully animals still thrive in this intensively farmed landscape. I love to watch them on fine spring evenings feeding alongside displaying partridges and pheasants, although the fast growing cereal crops will soon obscure their activities. Boxing is often associated with 'mad March hares', however, it occurs from January to late summer. Usually being hidden from view, at first by darkness then by taller crops. Boxing is not, as is often popularly supposed, males fighting, but the reaction of a female, who is not ready, to mate to an over persistent male.

I visited some superb hare fields early in 1996. Towards late evening they would appear as if by magic, although in reality they were rising from their daytime 'forms', which are shallow depressions in the ground in which they lie up. Unlike their cousin the rabbit they rely on lightening speed rather than underground safety.

I sat in the same section of hedgerow each evening and watched them through a telescope, although if you are down wind and keep totally still they will sometimes come surprisingly close. Watching them feeding, grooming and chasing is ample reward for the long hours spent sitting in this open, draughty countryside where the icy wind is enough to 'cut you in half'.

Roding Woodcock

The roding woodcock bridges the gap between the day's activity and that of the night. It is a strange time, close to dusk, waiting beside a small willow and ash clump surrounded by mature oaks and beech. This particular early April evening is cool and overcast and there is very little in the way of bird song except for the soft cooing of woodpigeons. Chiffchaffs, as they frequently do at this time of evening, have broken into bouts of nervous calling, contact calls rather than their more familiar song. Roosting cock pheasants shout out territorial messages to rivals and neighbours from high up in the ilex oaks and ivy covered boughs. Suddenly a song thrush shatters the calm with rich repeated phrases while a nearby dunnock shuffles around the dense dark canopy of a small holly, where it will spend the night.

This evening the woodcock are about early for I have already seen at least two roding birds. For me this display flight is quite magical, as these normally secretive birds perform their song flights just above the treetops on slowed down wings whilst sounding high pitched whispers and frog-like croaks. The bill is sometimes opened quite wide when calling and at times you can see their long tongues. Often the tails are half fanned and they will drop their legs and feet clear of the undertail as they produce the croaking calls. Occasionally one will pass right overhead calling and I was surprised how loud these calls can sound. One bird bobs his head from side to side trying to work out what the dark shadow watching from below is doing. It is difficult to work out just how many birds are displaying over this same area for I have seen at least five individuals. Some were easy to recognise from ragged holes in their wings where they have narrowly escaped the winter guns. From time to time a chase will break out between two birds, it is difficult to decide whether these are courtship chases or territorial disputes but they are definitely great to watch as the two birds weave at high speed through the trees sounding a high pitched chatter. The fevered activity seems to wane as darkness comes and the tawny owls steal the show.

James McCallum   9 April 96   Stiffkey.

Hares and a pair of grey partridges.

40

Hares and courting pheasants.

Sleeping spoonbills suddenly wake to scratch, preen and stretch, before flying off to feed.

May

May is a hectic month with the breeding season in full swing and the volume and variety of summer migrants increasing daily. Male whitethroats, having arrived, established territories and built several nests are frantically displaying and singing. They are hoping to entice a mate from an overnight arrival of females. Their antics become fevered as they perform 'butterfly' song flights above a prospective mate. The male tries to show his range of nests by singing from, around or even inside them. The nests are very rough and ready, you can see daylight through the bottom! However, the females seem easily pleased and one will eventually be selected for egg laying. Nearby their smart cousin the lesser whitethroat sings from the dense canopy of a line of hawthorns.

Newly arrived turtle doves give away their presence by their gentle, purring song. These beautiful doves have declined alarming as a breeding species over the last decade, especially on the coastal strip. It is a rare sight now to see them perform elegant display flights over high hedges and commons or to see the male strutting around a hen with his neck feathers pushed out into a large ruff. Another new arrival is the garden warbler singing from deep inside a woodland thicket. The song is remarkably similar to the blackcap, which inhabits similar areas, but seems more scratchy and chattering. Occasionally glimpsed, it is an unassuming bird with no striking features, being coloured only in delicate shades of warm and cold greys and browns. These combined with its large dark eye give it a modest, appealing character. There is another newly arrived migrant here too, also dull in colour but bright in personality, a spotted

Red-backed Shrike

flycatcher. Its greatest assets are spectacular aerobatics as it darts from a perch to catch airborne insects.

In the towns and villages parties of swifts are sounding their high-pitched shrieks over the pantiles. Amongst these new arrivals earlier migrants and some resident species are already on eggs or tending young. On the coast bearded tits and bitterns have young to feed. Willow warblers are weaving neat cup-shaped nests on the ground below the brambles by the second week of the month. Their close relative the chiffchaff, having arrived earlier, will already have eggs or young.

It always seems strange to see members of the same species at different stages of breeding or their journeys at the same location. For instance on the beaches our ringed plovers have their first chicks whilst nearby on the mud-flats are large groups of the same species en-route to breeding sites much further north. These birds have stopped on passage to build up much-needed fat reserves to fuel them on the next leg of their colossal journeys. Other passage waders are in abundance too. Sanderlings stop off for a few days on the beaches, dunlins gather in large groups on the mudflats, whilst on the marshes wood and common sandpipers, greenshanks and ruff mingle with the peewits and avocets. Of course there will always be the odd surprise during this month to add to the tempo and to test your field knowledge. The small wader with the dunlin, a bit distant and against the light. A stint but is it a little or a Temminck's? Suddenly a small group of spoonbills appears to land on a nearby lagoon or a handsome male red-backed shrike is hawking for bumblebees from its bramble lookout.

Male whitethroat

A group of black-tailed godwits. The dominant bird of this flock sees off another that has been feeding too close. The depressed half-spread tail is a threat posture common to many waders.

46

A stoat which has been hunting a fresh marsh returns with a field vole. It is also a frequent predator of eggs and young of ground nesting birds and its progress across the marsh can be followed by the anxious waders. The godwits hover above it continuously while the lapwings and redshank dive bomb it or follow on foot.

1st May 95   Great Sandy Low   from a flock of around 30   morning

A strong head wind forced these yellow wagtails to stop off for a few days in some coastal dunes. Just before the wind eased and allowed them to continue their journey the flock built up to over a hundred birds.

Late evening and a barn owl carries prey back to its nest amid a flock of swifts feeding on swarming insects above the reeds.

The drumming snipe performs best on warm, damp evenings.

Newly arrived garganey. I watched this pair displaying and mating in the late afternoon.

Courting common terns.

This Slavonian grebe is a unexpected find in a drainage dyke.

June

Although some birds will have long finished nesting, or in a few cases not yet started, the beginning of this month is the height of the breeding season. The success rate of nesting attempts and the survival rate of the young will be governed by numerous factors, the most influential being the weather. Periods of cold, wet and windy conditions can be disastrous for newly hatched or very small young and will frequently influence the amount of food that the parents can provide.

If strong winds are coupled with high tides, nesting terns and waders have the additional danger of their nests being washed away. However, if the weather is kind this can occasionally result in a bumper breeding year with good fledgling successes and, providing their habitats remain stable, can be enough to sustain their population levels despite experiencing several poor seasons.

The month opens with the first sandwich tern eggs hatching within the remote terneries at the sea's edge. Shelducks have brought their newly hatched broods from their nests in rabbit burrows to feed in the saltmarsh creeks. Due to the presence of large gulls in the area the chances of the ducklings surviving here are low, other pairs nesting in gaps in farmland straw stacks fare much better and several small broods or crèches can be seen on quiet farmland pools or larger lakes.

In the coastal reedbeds bearded tits begin their second broods and small noisy parties of tawny and black-striped fledglings from the earlier broods clamber up reed stems before launching themselves over the reedheads. Nearby the food flights of bitterns increase in frequency as the nestlings get bigger. Then, one day they will

Little Tern

suddenly cease indicating that the young have become mobile and are travelling with their mother on foot.

A whitethroat tends to its newly-hatched young inside a thick bramble, hawthorn and rough grassy corner where a field boundary and a drainage ditch meet. Below them a grey partridge also has newly-hatched chicks. On approach I am instantly made aware of this by the antics of both sets of parents as they try to lead me away from their young with elaborate distraction displays. The whitethroat flutters pathetically through the tangle with both wings spread, appearing very weak and easy to catch, whereas the partridge has a broken wing and is in great distress as it flutters and frantically calls, frequently jumping into the air in failed attempts to fly away. Aware of the situation I rapidly make myself scarce while the two birds, miraculously cured, sheepishly return to their young.

Close by a couple of quails are calling from a barley field. They have recently arrived on the front of a high pressure system that has spread warm weather and winds up from north Africa and the Mediterranean. Riding this warm air can be large immigrations of insects which follow the coastline in a constant stream. Often the most numerous being painted lady butterflies and silver y moths with lesser numbers of large and small whites and the occasional clouded yellow butterfly.

The return passage of green sandpipers and spotted redshanks begins in the second week, whilst adult curlews start to arrive at their traditional moulting areas within the saltings. They have already left their summer breeding haunts and serve to remind us to make the most of our short summer.

Turtle doves.

Raptors

I admire sparrowhawks, their powerful and skillful flight is always good to watch and when you have the good fortune to see one perched they are very attractive birds. Although often regarded as a hunter of wood and farmland birds, the individuals which hunt the saltmarshes have exploited the cover of suaeda bushes to surprise their prey and have developed skills to catch wading birds. I have seen them catch, or put them off an impressive list of waders. Redshanks are possibly the most frequently caught, one redshank, having dived underwater in an attempt to escape was taken in true 'fish eagle' style from just underneath the surface. One particular female hawk made a real nuisance of itself by catching ringed plovers which were brooding their eggs, surprising them from the cover of the suaeda bushes. Other waders caught include dunlin, knot, lapwing and even woodcock and jack snipe. One female flew out of some pine trees across the saltmarsh to catch a knot from amongst a flock of five hundred birds. Fortunately for the knot it managed to escape from the sparrowhawk's grip minus a handful of feathers, but the hawk's ability to single out an individual bird from a tight moving flock was extremely skillful.

These tactics are over shadowed by the sheer speed and power of a hunting peregrine. A bird, having been sitting out on some tidal sands, was put up by a passing helicopter. It preceded to soar upwards and drift away from the feeding grounds of the waders. This was a tactic I had seen before so I decided to keep watching it. It now changed direction and began to fly strongly and diagonally towards a mixed cloud of panic stricken waders. I was astonished to watch it overtake the flock, when it would have seemed easy to take one of its

choice, only to perform a u-turn and meet the moving flock head on, kicking a knot out of the air with its talons. The falcon circled then landed on its catch, feathers were soon streaming in a line across the mudflats carried by a gentle breeze. After all the commotion it is always surprising to watch how quickly the waders settle down once the peregrine is perched up and are often feeding close by.

A male sparrowhawk has caught and killed a young starling and begins to pluck it. He is continually mobbed by an anxious cock blackbird who has young nearby.

Summer reedbed

Warm sunshine and a gentle breeze cause the old dead reed stems to 'hiss', a noise with some qualities of the distant roar of the calming sea. In many ways this expanse of cold and warm grey stems looks not dissimilar to a calm ocean with small waves caused by gentle gusts of wind. Below these dead stems this year's growth of lush green leaves and new stems form a dense jungle inhabited by numerous reed warblers, sedge warblers and bearded tits. These birds are all busy feeding their rapidly growing broods on the abundance of wainscot moth caterpillars, these in turn feed on the reeds.

The bearded tits are already well into their second broods, as several fully-grown independent young are to be seen clambering up or flying above the reeds. Occasionally a bittern flops low over the reed bed. These are, at the moment, irregular feeding flights by a female with very small young. The male, having mated with her, feels that he has done his part and has disappeared to another area of marsh leaving his mate to bring up their young alone. Indeed she will not tolerate his presence anywhere near to the nest site.

Bitterns always look far more primitive than herons, especially in flight. This latest food flight sees her returning, black-faced and chested, her feathers wet and matted together with thick eel or fish slime. Judging from her condition more likely from a wrestle with the former. A black-headed gull, unhappy with her sudden appearance, continually 'mobs' her. On approaching the nest site she gives an angry shout before crashing into the reeds. The following events, hidden by reeds, I can only guess at for mystery is the trademark of the bittern.

Oystercatchers feeding chicks. Unlike other waders, whose chicks are independent from hatching, these young oystercatchers are dependent on their parents for food. It is not unusual to see fledged young begging and being fed.

These treecreepers had made their nest inside a deep crevice in the bark of a rotten Corsican pine stump. Watching from a good distance way, through tripod-mounted binoculars, it was possible to watch the family behaving freely and undisturbed. The young were already beginning to clamber to the top of the stump when I first saw the nest and there were some fantastic moments when the parents coaxed their six young into taking their first flights. Soon afterwards the family disappeared deep into the woodland.

Dabchicks with young amongst crowfoot and hornwort.

Non-breeding oystercatchers at their high tide roost. As the tide begins to ebb the roosting birds become restless and commence preening, stretching, scratching and yawning before disappearing to feed on the newly exposed feeding grounds.

July

The rewards for all the hardships of this year's breeding season become apparent this month. Sights and sounds of young birds dominate the countryside. The adults begin to show signs of wear and tear from tending to the ceaseless demands for food from their young. As the young develop and become independent the adults begin to moult their worn feathers. This is done in stages and is particularly noticeable in the flight feathers where small symmetrical gaps can be seen on each wing or side of the tail. Here a new feather will grow to replace the moulted one and the whole process will be staggered, ensuring that the birds do not become flightless. However, some birds such as ducks will shed a large area of flight feathers at the same time, rendering them capable of only flapping short distances. Instead they rely on the safety of open water or dense waterside vegetation. The drakes temporarily exchange their exquisite colours and markings for a more female-like camouflage dress during this period, which goes under the attractive name of 'eclipse'.

Many songbirds become silent and reclusive during this period of moult. But it is not just the adult birds that renew their feathers at this time of year. The young birds generally speaking will keep their new, neat set of flight feathers but will begin to replace many of their body feathers. The whole process of moult is a complex science and each species and age group within it will have its own pattern peculiar to themselves.

A little tern brings whitebait to newly fledged young.

The highly productive bearded tits will begin a third brood this month. Some have even been recorded having four broods in a single summer. Incredibly, juveniles from early broods have been known to breed that same season. Later in the autumn many of these birds flock up and disperse over vast distances to seek out new reedbeds. They are very susceptible to hard winters, so continually spreading to new areas ensures the species a greater chance of survival.

The young marsh harriers are now on the wing and spend long periods practising new, and fine tuning recently mastered manoeuvres. One bird chases a hare across the fresh marsh, the hare performs sudden changes in direction and the young harrier does its best to keep up. This chase is more for practice and fun, both parties seem aware of this and genuinely appear to enjoy it. From time to time one of their parents will arrive with prey. This is handed over by way of a beautifully executed aerial food pass. The young birds are frequently seen to be practising this manoevre with each other as part of their flying lessons.

The gregarious nature of young starlings and pied wagtails brings them together in large post-breeding flocks. They gather to feed in fields and pastures and big flocks can be seen on the coast. The wagtails preferring the beaches and tidelines and the starlings the saltings.

Also on the seashore the first young little and common terns are on the wing within the first week. The larger Sandwich terns require a week longer to develop and the first young are usually airborne at the beginning of the second week.

Whitebait and sandeels form their staple diet and their parents continue to feed them for sometime while the young birds learn and practice fishing. Large shoals of mackerel have moved into our coastal waters and are also feeding on the whitebait and sand eels. These larger fish are in turn followed and hunted by wandering groups of gannets and the occasional porpoise. The activity of the feeding terns draws in the first returning arctic skuas, which harass them until they release their catches. When you begin to piece together the chain of events that holds these mixed groups together the viewing becomes highly entertaining.

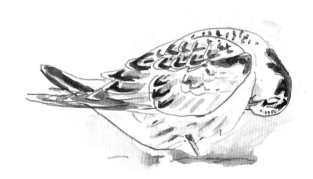

Juvenile Little Tern

The return passage of waders that have finished breeding is a big feature of the month. The adult birds arrive first and look fantastic in their summer finery. Dunlins with their black bellies and rufous backs gather in increasing numbers on the mudflats. Lesser numbers of knot, bar-tailed godwits and the occasional curlew sandpiper look handsome with brick-red bodies and brown chequered backs. The chestnut, black and white tortoiseshell patterned turnstones and rusty-throated sanderlings look so different from their more familiar, plainer winter dress.

On the saltmarsh the groups of moulting curlews have built up towards four figures. The smaller whimbrel are passing overhead in 'v' formations, sounding their characteristic seven-note whistle. Others have stopped off to feed on the marshes. A greenshank can be heard calling high up from a north-easterly direction and the return calls from birds feeding in small, loose parties in wide saltmarsh creeks sees it rapidly lose altitude as it calls back to them. Then, at the last minute it changes its mind and carries on south-westwards, the momentum of migration forcing it onwards. Common sandpipers have stopped off in the same saltmarsh creeks as the greenshanks. They feel the migratory urge too and gather together at dusk in tight noisy flocks. Their excited calls ring out as they weave through the channels at high speed, then suddenly they are off.

On the fresh marsh small groups of snipe, green and wood sandpipers, ruff, black-tailed godwits and spotted redshanks take their places alongside the breeding waders and waterfowl.

In the middle of the month the first fresh-feathered juvenile dunlin stands out amongst the black-bellied adults. Its arrival marks the start of the passage of young birds and a large increase in the volume and pace of the wader passage.

Fledgling little terns recovering after a sand storm.

64

Saltmarsh flora in hazy July afternoon sunshine.

1st July 95
Landing Ridge
hazy sun & cool NE.

Ringed plover with newly hatched chicks.

66

Young little and common terns.

As the tide ebbs a big shoal of whitebait is trapped in some tidal pools. As soon as the water becomes shallow enough, the gulls begin a feeding frenzy.

68

Resting greater black-backed gulls, common seals and sanderlings at low tide.

Great black-backed gulls establishing the feeding right to a tide line corpse of a young porpoise.

70

A mirage of cormorants on the horizon of sea and sky. This phenomenon can occasionally be experienced with the aid of a telescope and can add another dimension to sea watching!

August

The height of the holiday season and the warm weather sees large numbers of people heading for the beaches. But these are not the only visitors that flock to our coast. The wader passage is in full swing and several species are at their peak levels. The time to watch them is in the early morning or late evening, otherwise your viewing will be reduced to shimmering blobs lost in the heat haze, quite interesting from an artistic point though. Grey plovers gather on the mudflats and on distant undisturbed tidal sands. The summer adult's black face and silver spangled back make them one of the most attractive of all British birds. Golden plover pass through at high speed and a handful pause to rest briefly on sand bars or meadows. Equally handsome as their grey cousins, their backs this time being gold spangled whereas their face and underparts are often more freckled, especially in the southern populations.

Ruff and black-tailed godwits are in good numbers on the fresh marsh and the curlew flocks reach their highest levels. On the saltings small, loose parties of redshank arrive to join the breeding populations and spend most of their time feeding in saltmarsh creeks and lagoons.

The second half of the month sees the appearance of the first migrant landbirds. Willow warblers, wheatears and whitethroats are the usual pioneers.

Grey Plover

Redstarts, whinchats and pied flycatchers soon follow and when joined by a wryneck or a young red-backed shrike confirms that they are of continental, probably Scandinavian, origin. As with all migratory birds the weather has a great influence on their progress. Here it is typically east winds and rain that call a halt to proceedings and can result in large numbers of passerines being grounded. A closer look can sometimes reveal the odd surprise and it is worth looking out for the large, thickset barred warbler in the coastal elders or the more athletic icterine warbler with its neat yellow throat and pale wing panel.

It is not only passerines that appear during these conditions, a second glance amongst the wheatears feeding in a low stony plateau in the sand dunes sees a larger bird, well camouflaged against the grey lichens, sand and flint gravel. A wader with a dark cap and a broad white stripe over each eye meeting in a 'v' shape on its nape. This is a young dotterel from some remote mountain range, it is remarkably fearless and you almost feel that you are the first human it has set eyes on. However, birds are not the only airborne migrants to reach us and hot weather spreading up through Europe frequently sees large numbers of insects; moths, butterflies, hoverflies, bees, dragonflies and beetles. These mixed movements are quite common and in some years a particular species may invade the area in staggering numbers.

On the shore good numbers of terns have fledged and now gather on the sands in loose groups. The young are able to fend for themselves but still beg their parents for food and are indeed fed by them. Their family ties remain very strong and young birds will stay with at least one of the parents and when they feel the time is right for them to migrate southwards they will also leave as a unit. The dark presence of arctic skuas is now a regular feature of the seascape and several of these pirates have taken up temporary residence. They sit on the sea and wait for adult terns to return from fishing trips with food for their offspring. They spot the thin silver sliver carried in the tern's bill from some distance and rise up to intercept the bird. Both birds are skilfull in the air and some impressive and at times long-winded chases continue until one party gives in.

Strong onshore winds greatly increase the number of these skuas and if you are fortunate the smaller, more pelagic, long-tailed skua may be blown close inshore too. If your luck is really in it could be an adult bird complete with incredibly long tail-streamers, dusky belly and flanks and neat black cap. In such conditions it is worth keeping your eyes open for the black and white flashes of manx shearwaters among the thicker set grey and white fulmars. Less regularly seen are the long, thin, brown wings and body and the efficient mechanical wingbeats and steep shearing glides of the sooty shearwater. If the conditions are just right a great variety of seabirds can pass close to shore in good numbers. Make the most of these opportunities as these are rare spectacles which are over all too soon.

A fall of pied flycatchers, feeding on immigrant silver-y moths, on the fence of the famous Blakeney Point plantation.

Graylings and sand dunes – 17 August 1997

A scorching hot mid-August day in the coastal sand dunes. Down here in the hollows the heat really radiates and at times you almost feel as if you could suffocate. All around are the slow rasping calls of mottled grasshoppers and the short flights of grayling butterflies. These are two of my favourite insects, probably because I spend hours watching them on this short rabbit-grazed turf when it is too hot to do anything else. The graylings may not be the most showy butterflies but they have great character and an almost reptilian look about them!

Often when resting the graylings sit with wings closed, their forewings, except for the outer-tips, hidden by the hindwings. Their patterning matches the bare sand, lichen and dead grass so well that unless you watch them settle they can be very hard to see. They also have a habit of angling their bodies into the sun, this has a double effect in showing their camouflage markings off and also reducing their giveaway shadows. In fact they seem so self conscious of their shadows that if one lands on your arm you can fractionally move, then watch the butterfly react and adjust its body angle accordingly. A sudden movement or a passing insect will frequently induce them to flick up their forewings to show their 'eye-spots'. This marking, in common with other members of the butterfly family known as the browns, is a black spot with a white centre and has the effect of appearing to be the eye, complete with shining highlight, of a creature much bigger than itself.

In fact when involved with activities requiring intense concentration such as drawing, the sudden production of this 'eye' is enough to make you subconsciously freeze when you know all too well that it has been able to see you all along. However, when you find yourself foiled by this marking you realise how effective it can be as a form of defence by means of deception.

I watch a pair courting, the female slowly walking forward with wings almost fully spread frequently flapping with the male following very close behind, his wings closed. Suddenly they break into a towering chase fluttering upwards in tight circles. This is repeated several times before they go their separate ways still unmated.

Graylings

Grayling threat display towards a mottled grasshopper.

Migrant hawker
dragonflies resting
on brambles.

20 Aug 97
migrant - migrant Hawkers
resting after feeding

Dusk studies of hedgehogs.

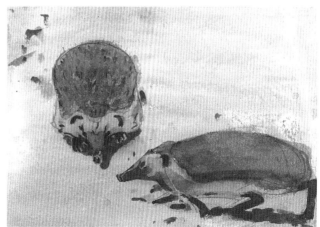

Ringed plover and turnstones at a high tide roost on the edge of the saltmarsh. The delicate paper thin seedheads of sea campion glow when backlit in the strong sunshine.

Studies of adult and newly-fledged ringed plovers.

Black, common, little and sandwich terns, kittiwake, sanderling and common seal. Unlike the other birds black terns are mainly a freshwater species and these migrating groups linger offshore to feed on swarms of ladybirds that are moving on a warm air current.

Painted lady butterflies hatching from pupae on the thistles that have escaped extensive topping and spraying. These are the offspring from a huge immigration of these insects from the previous June. I was surprised how quickly the process between emerging and flight was completed.

September

One of my favourite months. For me it has the real essence of autumn. People speak of being overwhelmed by a strong feeling of melancholy. This is very evident on still silent days of low soft sunshine when resident robins break into their mournful autumn song. But regardless of the mood or weather I enjoy everyday of this month.

The saltmarsh having long lost its lavender bloom takes on a rich patchwork of reds, pinks and purples of seablites and samphires. An earthy smell is all about the farmlands heightened by the first few frosty mornings.

Although I enjoy this moodiness, it is a month for birds. It is very hard to define the four seasons but this is a definite change-over month. Migration is in full flow as birds head for their chosen winter quarters. Summer visitors, passage migrants and winter visitors briefly rub shoulders. The return dates of winter, or for that matter summer, migrants are remarkably consistent. None more so than the brent and pink-footed geese. Over the last five or six years I have kept much more thorough notebooks and the returning dates are quite amazing. As a rule you look for brents and listen for pinkfeet. Brents always arrive back at their favourite feeding areas first, the closest area to me being the eelgrass beds of Wells Harbour. Between the 16th and 19th are the current favourite dates.

The pinkfeet arrive in from due south over Holkham calling. They then drop onto the grazing marshes west of Lady Anne's Drive. Over the last five years they have been incredibly consistent arriving between the 12th and 14th, usually on the latter date.

The return of other wintering birds, not being so obvious as the geese, are more difficult to observe. However, it is interesting to note how the dates of returning rock pipits often coincide with the arrival of brents.

It is usually this month that sees the first redwings, fieldfares, bramblings, shorelark, snow and Lapland buntings. Wigeon and teal increase strongly in numbers as the month progresses, as do the vast night-time gull roosts. Wintering and passage raptors are evident too, peregrines and merlins begin to take up permanent residence and the first hen harrier usually puts in an appearance around mid-month.

Weather conditions can have a dramatic effect on the progress of migrant birds. Strong onshore winds can force seabirds close providing good views of what would normally be strictly pelagic feeders. Whilst winds from a north or easterly direction mixed with rain or fog over Norfolk and fine weather over Scandinavia or eastern Europe can force exceptional numbers of migrating landbirds to be grounded on our coast. The groundings or 'falls' during September are famed for their great numbers and variety of species and have produced many unexpected visitors.

Siberian Thrush

Newly arrived brent geese on eel grass beds.

A young red-necked phalarope.

Young little stints and pied wagtails feed on a foamy lake shore during strong winds.

An osprey and a hobby choose the same dead tree to perch in and regard each other with curiosity. The pale edges to its back feathers and brown chest make the osprey a juvenile. The fiery-yellow eyes and large ruff of feathers on its nape give it a fearsome expression.

Huge numbers of black-headed and common gulls arrive at this time of year. Large groups feed inland but all return to roost on the coast at night. They frequently visit freshwater lakes to bathe and drink. Here a group arrive to wash amongst some coots, this is always a vigorous affair and appears to be a highly satisfying activity.

Young dunlin, ringed plover and curlew sandpiper feeding in samphire beds.

October

October in many ways is an extension of September with immigration and migration of birds dominating the landscape. September provides excitement in variety whereas in October it is the sheer number of birds moving that is most impressive.

The pinkfeet and brent geese strengthen in numbers and around mid-month the first juvenile brents begin to arrive with their parents in family groups. Wigeon and teal are still arriving, their numbers being swelled on the coastal grazing marshes. Some days you are met with musical barks coming from the north-east as a beautiful line of Bewick's swans arrives from the Arctic.

Large flocks of peewits and golden plover suddenly appear to brighten up the autumn farmland. The newly arrived golden plovers seem particularly edgy and unsettled with their new surroundings and frequently rise in tight formations before dropping back to feed again.

Movements of smaller birds can be spectacular too. Sometimes starlings and northern thrushes pour westwards through the coastline. The air is then full of noises, the 'whoosh' of starling wings as a tight flock passes low overhead, the harsh chatters and high squeals of fieldfares, whispering contact calls of redwings and high trills of migrating blackbirds. Mixed amongst them can be smaller groups of skylarks, bramblings, siskins and chaffinches. The calls of snow and Lapland buntings, shorelark and twite are heard more regularly as the month progresses. What are often regarded as garden birds are moving too, wrens, robins,

Young merlin in pursuit of a wheatear.

dunnocks, goldcrests, great and blue tits, even the occasional great spotted woodpecker and treecreeper are making the big journey south to milder climes. These movements are heightened by weather conditions. Onshore winds with light rain showers or mist and fog can produce breathtaking numbers. Migrants from much further east get blown off course too and soon become mixed in with these movements, increasing the excitement of the spectacle.

A Richard's pipit moves west along the dune ridges calling at frequent intervals, a great grey shrike pauses briefly on a hawthorn or a boldly marked yellow-browed warbler joins a group of goldcrests and chiffchaffs in the coastal sallows. These movements are awe inspiring to us, however, a walk along the tideline a few days later tells a different tale, wings and feathers of thrushes, starlings and smaller passerines are mixed in with storm washed tubes of peacock worms, sand masons, sea potatoes, razor shells and other tideline flotsam. These are hard times for migrating birds and it is worth remembering this when the skies are empty and coastal scrub quiet. It is these days that are good for the birds themselves, for they are already well on their way to completing a big chunk of their long hard journeys to their chosen winter quarters, unhindered by headwinds, rain, mist and fog.

However, not all birds view these harsh conditions as unfavourable. The big gulls and the raptors relish such occasions as tired migrants make easy pickings. The big gulls

are probably the most unsavoury killers, they think nothing of forcing thrushes into the sea where they will drown them and eat them whole, the raptors will at least kill them quickly. When all this coastal migration is in full swing raptors are probably at their most evident, indeed many of these are migrants too. With the abundance of prey they seem less territorial and more tolerant of each other. Merlins and sparrowhawks work the dunes and coastal marshes, tired migrants may be easy pickings, however, they have used much of their fat reserves on their long journeys so provide poor meals for the predators.

The silhouette of a hen harrier over saltmarshes and farmland becomes a more regular feature this month. There is also a regular change over of what could be assumed to be the same resident peregrine. For some days it is a young male then the next an adult female and so on. This is now the best month to see, what was only a few years ago a regular autumn and winter bird, the magnificent short-eared owl. The shape, markings, flight action, not forgetting the piercing stare from the yellow eyes, make it one of the most impressive sights to be encountered in north Norfolk.

Foiled by a rabbit burrow.

Fallow Deer

Late October is a favourite time to watch fallow deer as this is the beginning of the rut. There is a lot of noise and behaviour happening as the bucks try to gather as many does as possible. These were drawn in Holkham Park, an excellent place to watch them as they are reasonably tame and if you give them time and space they will perform well in front of you. It is good fun to call back at the roaring bucks, especially at dusk, as they quickly respond, and in the poor light will even charge until they catch sight or scent of you and do a quick u-turn and bolt off.

Fallow does.

Fallow bucks rutting.

Jack Snipe

The jack snipe is for me one of the most enigmatic of all our visitors. In north Norfolk they appear in small numbers as an autumn passage migrant, especially in October and November, as an uncommon winter resident and again as a scarce passage migrant in early spring.

After a time it is possible to get to know large areas of the countryside intimately and after even more time develop a feel for jack snipe country. I know of a series of favoured hideouts and they seem catholic in their choice of reedy, silt and cattle trodden marshy fields. My first ever encounter of one was from a hide at one of the famous nature reserves. However, for years after this I never managed to see anything other than a small, dark wader with a bright straw yellow, striped back rising almost at my feet. This was due to their habits and camouflage. Their neat yellow back stripes look so similar to the marsh vegetation that the birds seem conscious of this. So much so, that on your approach they adjust their body position and markings to blend in with the pattern of the surrounding vegetation, confident that they will not be seen and just sit tight until you pass. If your paths do cross they will fly up, but only when you are right on top of them. To see more than this I needed to develop a new approach. I realised that some of the best places to encounter them were where cattle had churned up patches of marsh and trampled and grazed reeds, sedges and rushes. The newly exposed rich, black silt were frequently covered by a network of footprints, probe-marks and fresh white droppings.

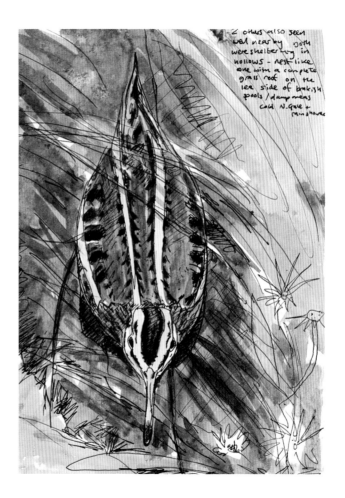

So following the example of the cattle and repeatedly trampling over the same area I made a couple of small, silty patches, making sure that there were enough dead reed stems present for the birds to hide amongst. I returned a couple of days later and using binoculars methodically searched over the area. Initially I saw nothing but then I noticed what appeared to be two symmetrical reed stems slightly richer in colour than the others. As I looked a jack snipe suddenly materialised from them. It was a great moment and a long ambition realised. Having secured my binoculars onto a small tripod I began to draw, noting its relatively short, broad-based bill, dark crown, straw-yellow head and back stripes. The pale body was marked with small dark bars and peppered with tiny blotches of various tones of browns, greys and pale yellows. When the sun broke through I was shocked to see a vivid green iridescence on the dark mantle and scapular feathers.

After some time, providing I kept still, it began to relax. Abandoning its camouflage posture, and fluffing its flank feathers over its closed wings, it began a peculiar mechanical bobbing motion before tucking its head away and sleeping. This action is not only fascinating but also characteristic, not to mention highly amusing.

I returned several times over the next few weeks and was frequently unsuccessful but I did have several other sightings and made further drawings that winter. I was beginning to get my eye in and have been fortunate to witness and paint several others since.

One of the best experiences to date was on a late October afternoon. I was taking a short cut across a marshy field when I almost trod on a jack snipe, in fact I felt it touch the toe of my boot. I was quite surprised at this, as although it is frequently stated in the literature, in my own experience they normally rise from a couple of metres ahead. It also dropped down again after flying only a short distance. This behaviour is also stated in the literature, however, the majority of birds I see fly a good distance before settling.

Anyway, a few days later a friend and I were crossing the same marsh and I mentioned that I had at long last seen a jack snipe that behaved as the text books said it should. I had no sooner said this when I noticed what was presumably the same bird sitting right at my feet. I whispered to my friend to carefully come over and we marvelled at it for some time. I slowly crouched down and it didn't so much as flinch, so reliant was it of its camouflage, despite the fact that I was only inches from it. I quietly announced that I was going to pick it up. My friend laughed. But to the surprise of both of us I slowly put my hand above, then in front of it, then slowly lowering it I gently picked it up. It was absolutely beautiful and we could appreciate some of its finer details such as its tiny spear shaped tail. Its iridescent bottle green gloss shone brightly and to a lesser extent a purple sheen could be seen too. I rested it in my palm and could see and feel its pale green-yellow legs push downwards as it jumped up to aid its take-off before dropping back into the marsh.

I went back again over the next two days and was fortunate to see it both times. I managed to get several paintings done without needing to get quite so close! The following day saw the start of a period of heavy rain and when I next returned the whole area as flooded and temporarily unsuitable for the jack snipe.

From my experience it would appear that some birds must be crepuscular or nocturnal in their feeding habits as they could often be found in the exact same places during the daytime over a period of several weeks. For example one wintering bird had made a small hollow amongst dead reed and sedge stems in between some grassy hummocks. Here it would rest and, judging from the amount of moulted feathers, preen itself. It could be found in this exact spot for over three weeks.

Recently I saw some interesting behaviour during a winter's day of northerly gales and rain showers. In an area of rough grazing and silty pools a couple of individuals were seen sitting in cup-shaped hollows with grass growing over the top in the form of a roof. All that could be seen of one bird was its head and bill, the rest of its body was inside the structure and hidden in shadow. These birds were sheltering from the harsh conditions and the cavities were presumably manipulated, if not entirely constructed, by the birds themselves.

Jack snipe.

98

Wood pigeons and skylarks on newly tilled fields.

Roosting Cormorants

A vast percentage of north Norfolk's cormorant population feed at sea or in shallow intertidal waters. At night time they congregate in large communal roosts in undisturbed tree-tops, usually surrounded by water. They have a highly complex visual and vocal behavioural repertoire. I spent several of my most fascinating and enjoyable periods spaced over several years at, what was at the time, the premier roost for the whole north Norfolk coast. Unfortunately these birds were deemed undesirable by many people and the roost trees were cut down and the birds scared off. I still mourn the loss of that spectacular roost which peaked at over four hundred birds but at least I still have fabulous memories and a huge volume of drawings and studies.

Shorelarks feeding on Holkham beach after a busy half-term holiday.

November

The pace of November is less hectic but the weather can be more varied. Famous November fogs, sharp frosts, crisp sunny days or mild damp ones. I sometimes think of it as a settling down month, winter migrants are usually well established and their populations have become more stable by the month's end. It is a good time for geese. White-fronts at Holkham and Burnham Overy are becoming a more obvious feature of the winter landscape. Pinkfeet numbers are building towards their peak. Amongst the brents the tell-tale white, 'sergeants stripes' on the backs of the young birds give an indication of this year's breeding success.

Shorelark, snow buntings, twite and rock pipits gather on the beaches, tidelines and saltmarshes in varying numbers and at different locations each year. At the time of writing, November 1998, it is the shorelark that has really stolen the limelight. Spectacular groups can be found all along the coast challenging the famous counts from the 1970s. Only this morning, before heavy rain set in, I was enjoying the visual and audible pleasures of a flock of two hundred and ten barely a mile from my home. They were feeding on samphire seeds with the magnificent Holkham Bay as a backdrop.

Cold weather can stimulate large movements of birds from the continent. Some days are dominated by vast numbers of wood pigeons moving in large oval flocks across the skyline. This is frequently a morning phenomenon and there is little evidence of them later in the day. This is often the best month for divers and grebes and, if combined with a period of high pressure that has calmed the sea, can enable some good observations of them feeding at length without losing them in the wave troughs. On the other end of the scale low pressure can pull in some rough weather and if it falls into a northerly quarter you soon get a good clue as to its origins. If you brave the elements and head for the sea again this too can produce another superb set of birds. If the temperature does not help you guess the wind's origins the birds will. Great and pomarine skuas moving in small groups, delicate little gulls amongst their larger cousins, the black lines of scoter are occasionally interrupted by the white wing flashes of velvet scoters. Long-tailed ducks and divers speed past, the latter on long thin wings with head and legs stretched out on either side.

Razorbills and guillemots move like bullets on short whirring wings. Their smaller relative, the charming little auk, can be storm-driven in good numbers. Their size and speed is so similar in manner to starlings and dunlins, which are also passing low over the sea, that it is not unusual for a singleton to join up with one of these flocks. In fact they fit in so well with the flow of the starlings that they don't always seem to realise that they have left the seashore and are now passing over arable fields or dune ridges.

These weather patterns also lead to the grounding of woodcocks or, if the wind has an easterly origin, exciting migrants can be seen.

Little Auk with Starling flock

Shorelarks and snow buntings.

November migrants – a memorable late autumn fall

11 November 1996

The morning started bright and clear, however the north-east wind had begun to freshen. As I left the house, around mid-morning, the horizon to the north and east was solid black and the first rain drops began to fall. I retreated back inside and a torrential downpour followed. I wouldn't be painting pinkfeet today. In half an hour the rain had stopped but the weather looked set for an afternoon of squally showers.

Determined not to waste the day, I decided to have a walk around the coastal marshes to see if any migrant birds had been grounded by the weather. I greatly enjoy the migration periods, especially in late autumn. I always watch the same small areas of coastline, instead of rushing around the whole of north Norfolk, for only by watching these same areas can you begin to understand a little more about what time of year different birds are migrating and which weather is the best to encounter them. With nature nothing is guaranteed, there are always surprises and it is this that makes migration so exciting.

So with waterproofs and thigh boots on I began to wade across the tidal channels and jump saltmarsh creeks. After a couple more heavy showers and a stunning rainbow, I finally arrived at

Great grey shrike with goldcrest.

the first trees. Blackbirds were passing overhead in small groups giving their delicate ringing contact calls, which were in direct contrast to the loud chattering alarm calls given by others rising from the brambles as I walked past. Smaller numbers of redwings were here too, their alarm calls were an even harsher chatter while their migrating calls were higher pitched whispers. These northern thrushes are truly wild when they first reach our shores and were particularly nervous as two sparrowhawks were working the area.

A chiffchaff, keeping low in the brambles, was actively searching for insects and would frequently dart up into the sycamores. It was quite tame and looked really attractive with a neat set of new feathers and and smart black legs and bill. Moving on, the first of the hoped for woodcocks rose from close by. A dozen or more were to follow, all seen in flight as they were flushed from nearby cover, their camouflage too good for my eyes. A sharp tacking call came from the next clump of brambles, my money was on blackcap or lesser whitethroat. A large grey warbler with a neat black cap joined a couple more, all fluffed up trying to scrape a meal from the last remenants of the season's blackberry crop.

Next came a group of goldcrests, finger tame, as new arrivals often are. Barely over three inches from bill tip to tail, I am always amazed to think that they have just crossed the North Sea and wonder how many must perish in these harsh conditions. I once saw one come in over the sea, it must have been so tired because it dropped onto the beach just in front of the breakers, only to be swallowed by the next wave before I could reach it. They are certainly one of my favourites with their almost innocent and, at times, even confused-looking expressions. In amongst this flock was their showy cousin the firecrest. I had heard him calling earlier, the call is very similar to the goldcrest but slightly stronger and more buzzing. This one was a shocking male with bright orange crown, black and white striped head and a lovely bronze patch at its shoulder. It was really turning into a memorable visit and I still had another group of trees to come. Blackbirds were still passing overhead and the occasional brambling and snow bunting were moving too.

In the last trees a larger group of goldcrests had gathered in a loose flock of around twenty five birds and with them, low down in the tree, was a real treat. A warbler with clean white underside, green upperparts marked with yellow stripes on its wings, above its eyes and through its crown. This was a Pallas's warbler from the Siberian forests. I watched it for some time feeding in low pines with the similar sized goldcrests. At one point it flew up into a small sycamore to join a couple of goldcrests hovering underneath the large yellow leaves delicately picking off tiny insects. When hovering it displayed yet another yellow marking, a square across its lower back.

It was time to head home, I just wanted a quick look over the dune crest to see the seascape. The tide was going to be flowing soon. These were big marsh tides, and, backed by a strengthening north-east

Desert Wheatear

wind, not to be messed with. The sea was really white and another squall was coming through. Then, whilst jogging up a small ridge, I was to get an even bigger surprise, for rising from the base of a small pine to hover then land in front of me was a really boldly patterned bird. A pale, grey-brown wheatear with a black face, legs and tail. The wings were dark as well, with pale lacy edges. This was a desert wheatear from central Asia. He flitted across to another area of dunes flashing his black tail, I could just make out a tiny patch of white where the tail met its sandy rump and the wings showed large pale patches. Then he was off over the beach and away. After a brief search I failed to relocate him. I really had to get back before the tide moved, and besides I was starting a new evening job and couldn't be late on my first night!

The weather on the following day was foul, a fierce north-east gale with heavy rain. I ventured out for a few hours but it was really a day to stay indoors. The thirteenth was altogether better, the wind was dropping off and the sky brightening as the morning went on. I cycled down to the pinewoods at Wells beach with high expectations, but after a couple of hours walking through the pines I was surprised at the lack of migrants present. However, as I was leaving a single quiet ''teck'' call came from low dense brambles. With time and a keen interest, the subtle differences between "tic", "teck" and "tack" calls of small passerines can almost become a second language. This particular call was somewhere between the "check" of a wren and the hard "tack" of a lesser whitethroat.

I suspected dusky warbler, another siberian migrant I have had the good fortune to bump into and watch at length in this area before. These single notes are used as a contact calls but if you approach too closely the birds became more agitated and call repeatedly and much louder. This one did just that, then appeared in some low vegetation, chiffchaff sized but looking slightly shorter tailed and more stocky. Dressed in a mixture of grey browns and off whites they may not be the most colourful of warblers but have an attractive character and habits. A friend of mine appeared close by and I called him over. Amazingly, as we watched, a second dusky warbler started calling behind us and we soon had superb views of both birds. This second one had a new silver ring on one leg and we later found out that it had been caught in a mist-net close by on the caravan site during the big arrival on the eleventh.

During the afternoon I visited the same area of dunes and pines where I had seen the pallas's warbler and desert wheatear . Not surprisingly very few birds remained in these exposed pines, though a beautiful tiercel peregrine was reward enough for the effort.

14 November 1996

A clear sunny morning with light winds saw many birds re-orientating themselves and passing along the coast. I teamed up with a friend and we walked along the marsh at Stiffkey. Thrushes, skylarks, finches and buntings were moving westwards and 56 snipe moving in groups of up to 17 was exceptional. My friend Andy, keen to see a Pallas's warbler was left feeling very frustrated having picked one up calling from a huge, thick gorse clump but failing to get a view. I walked onto Morston and he turned back. Meeting up later I had very little to report but he had seen a great grey shrike moving along the hedgerows and a 'Denchman' – a hooded crow, over the saltmarsh.

I went home for some dinner but Andy, determined to find a Pallas's warbler, went to Holkham Pines, a well-known site for these rare visitors. I met up with him in the car park as he was leaving for work. His search had been fruitless despite knowing all the best areas. I still had an hour or so before I too had to leave for work. He suggested that I have a look in a small clump of birch and bramble nearby. As I walked down the track a large party of tits and goldcrests were moving through the trees, I had to smile for in front of me only feet away in a small ilex oak was his quarry. The warbler soon passed through with the fast moving flock and all was silent again. Silent except for that "teck" call again. I couldn't believe my ears or eyes as a dusky warbler appeared in the low brambles. We returned the next day, Andy was in luck, the Pallas's warbler was present along with a second bird. Better views of the dusky warbler showed it to be the same ringed bird from the other end of the pines, its companion was to be seen in the same area, both having moved a mile through acres of seemingly identical habitat to settle here. This concluded the end of an incredible and magical week.

Pallas's Warbler

106

Dusky warbler.

Woodcock arrivals

The woodcock, along with jack snipe and bittern, really capture my imagination. Their camouflage and retiring ways make observation very difficult and for me leave them shrouded in mystery. Over several years of looking you may be lucky in gaining some fascinating insights into their lives. However, it is definitely a case of the more you learn the less you know.

Woodcock can only be described as a scarce breeding bird in north Norfolk with few woods and estates having roding birds. It is in the late autumn and winter that they really come into their own. The first signs of their arrival are usually in early October when they begin to leave their breeding grounds in northern Europe and move south for the winter. They are however a distinctly nocturnal migrant and it is only adverse weather, a northerly head wind with mist or rain that will ground them on this coast in any numbers, giving us a clue to the huge numbers that must pass through these shores. In fact naturalists and wildfowlers at the end of the last century and the beginning of this one used to write enthusiastically about when the first 'woodcock moon' of October was coupled with northerly winds. Then they could watch them come in over the sea to drop into the coastal sand dunes so tired that they would fall asleep instantly and could even be picked up.

This immigration continues throughout late autumn, the numbers moving in winter are governed by the onset of cold weather in central Europe. My most memorable woodcock arrival to date was on the 2 November 1995 in a thin half-mile stretch of coastal sand dunes and pine trees. I had visited the same area the previous day and three woodcock were present, however, that afternoon the wind turned north-west and strengthened then a series of showers followed. A lot of blackbirds and redwings were grounded, so the next day I returned with a friend to see what else had arrived during the night. My diary for that day reads:

Woodcock, a minimum of 80 throughout the pines and in the dunes. Many favouring the cover of the pines, 14 alone were put out from the base of a clump of dozen two to three foot high pines. Several were seen on the ground, two in particular giving amazing views. They often gave away their presence by the shine of their eyes. One seen well in an open patch froze to the spot so we crawled down to get some excellent views, when we retreated it eventually moved with very slow leg movements and a mechanical bobbing motion. Feeling more confident it then ran off into the marram and pine tangle. We crawled after it and came across another much darker and more heavily marked individual, with a noticeably shorter bill. Initially this bird was actually sitting hunched up asleep with its bill tucked away. As we crawled right up to it, it awoke with a jump, drawing its feathers tight and dropping down onto its legs, now ready for the spring loaded launch into flight.

Of course an arrival of woodcock of this magnitude would not be complete without the presence of a 'woodcock owl' or two. Although this name is usually given to the short-eared owl, two long-eared owls put out of the dense pines were well received. One headed out across the salt marsh, the other landed high in the breezy pines, the wind blowing its ear-tufts about. Two little auks flying westwards along the beach landed briefly on the beach, rounding off a remarkable day. The winter of 1995/6 turned out to be one of the best for woodcock in living memory. Although considered notoriously difficult to shoot, around two hundred were shot during hard weather in less than a week on one local estate. Although unforgivable, it gives us some idea of the numbers present, probably running into the thousands. The several local estate owners who will not let woodcock be shot on their estates, appreciating their hard winter life and long migrations, have my complete respect.

A woodcock surprised whilst feeding in dense bramble understorey. It reacts by cocking and fanning its tail, before running clear and flying off.

'Woodcock moon' - this one having a double halo. The following night saw this moon coupled with strong onshore winds and a good number of woodcock were indeed grounded and could be found in coastal sand dunes and woodland early the next morning.

Long-eared Owl.

Late November morning

A late November morning of hazy but bright sun, however the wind was ice cold. I needed a change from sheltering in hedgerows of large exposed fields where beet had recently been harvested and the unwanted tops left behind. For these are the places to wait for and hopefully sketch pinkfeet. I decided to cycle over to Stiffkey to draw some rock pipits which I had seen a few days earlier. They had been feeding on a thick belt of saltmarsh tangle washed up by marsh tides and a north-east gale. As I reached the top of the sea wall I realised my mistake, the tide was out so the pipits would have acres of muddy creeks to feed in. Rock pipits always have an excuse why they are not present, the tide is either too high or too low or the mud is better on the far side of the channel. Making them, for me, one of the most difficult birds to comfortably sketch even though they are a fairly common winter visitor to the saltmarshes.

Still there's always something else to see. A high pitched call followed by an electric blue flash from the base of a sluice gate, there is a redshank and a gang of dunlin and ringed plover on the mud, so tucked beside a suaeda bush I sit sketching them hoping the kingfisher will return for it is not the first time I've surprised it from this perch.

Soon the waders are scattered by a couple of dog walkers, I am beginning to think this is not going to be my day but as I am clearing up to go a group of dabchicks surface by the sluice gate.

I spend an hour or so with them, watching them alternate between bouts of intensive fishing to periods of relaxing and dozing. They idle in the slack water in the alcoves of the sluice gate wall or the remnants of its predecessor – a line of twisted branches, their neat square edges worn away over the years, revealing scaled down versions of their original tree shapes. Dozing with their bills and foreheads tucked into their breast feathers there is a constant flashing shine from their dark eyes. It is amusing to watch the transformation from these resting 'powder puffs' to small sleek feather-tight fishing birds.

The waders having slowly returned are up again in alarm, the redshanks, as usual the noisiest. I just catch sight of the culprit, a young merlin, as it flips over the sea wall. Wader calls are echoed on the fresh marsh with the additions of peewit, snipe, skylark, yellowhammer and the odd lapland bunting for good measure. I am feeling the cold so it's time to make a move, the dabchicks follow suit, leaving only a series of ripples and bubbles.

Dabchick

During the winter many dabchicks move from inland lakes, ponds and ditches to sheltered coastal waters.

November fogs: migrating thrushes, tired and disorientated, literally fall out of the sky when their contact calls are replied to from the safety of coastal pines which were hidden below them.

114

Antagonism between two large pink-footed goose families during thick fog.

*A drake pochard joins some others loafing alongside
tufted and ruddy ducks and a dabchick.*

Waterfowl rising. The pochard run along the surface to aid their take-off, while the mallard rise straight from the surface, the female being smaller, lighter and more nimble often gets airborne first.

December

By the time December is upon us we are rapidly moving towards mid-winter. The journeys and migrations of the majority of species are complete and the winter scene in north Norfolk is more or less established. This time of year allows you to relax and enjoy the winter wildlife and landscape in detail. The peak counts of wildfowl occur, with spectacular flocks of wigeon, teal, mallard and pintail on the grazing marshes and wetlands. Numbers of pinkfeet and brent geese have also peaked. Tens of thousands of pinkfeet arrive at their traditional night-time roost sites, on undisturbed tidal sands, in vast skeins at dusk. Their dawn departures are just as impressive as they fly deep into the surrounding countryside to feed in fields where sugar beet has been harvested and the leaves and tops of this root crop left behind. It is the root tops that these geese seek out, and the pattern of harvesting will dictate their movements.

The white-fronts favour the grasses of the grazing marshes, preferring the drier fields. In contrast to the other geese they arrive later in the season with peak numbers in the new year. Even then the flocks only number in hundreds. However, the sight of the mature birds with their dazzling white foreheads, heavy velvet-black barring across their bellies and the rich orange legs are one of the highlights of the winter.

On the beaches and marshes the wintering passerines begin to favour certain feeding areas. Using a bit of fieldcraft, and selecting a sheltered spot, it is possible to get prolonged close views of snow buntings, twite and shorelarks, without unnecessarily disturbing them. The beaches can get busy with people on fine days and these birds can find it difficult to feed without being disturbed, so it is important not to unsettle them.

Hard weather in continental Europe can influence the winter scene here. This often results in influxes of several species, the most visible being lapwings, woodpigeons and starlings. Goosanders and smew sometimes turn up on coastal drains and on inland lakes. Other species arrive too but may be less conspicuous in their habits. In the marshes water rails are encountered more regularly as is the occasional immigrant bittern. Snipe appear in good numbers in the damp areas of rough marshes. Here, where rich black silt gathers, they are joined by their close relative the jack snipe. Woodcock, although similar in appearance, are woodland birds, here they can be found amongst the bramble understorey especially in damp woods and copses.

Snow Bunting

Shorelarks feeding on samphire seeds towards dusk on one of the shortest days of the year.

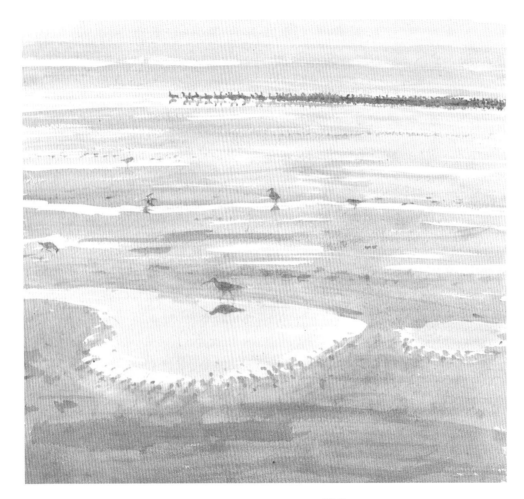

At dawn the pinkfeet often walk along the distant tidal sands in a long, thin line before taking flight.

A guillemot 'flies' through shallows feeding on shrimps that it disturbs from their hiding places under the sand. A black-headed gull follows in the air above, ready to pounce on anything missed.

Oystercatcher, dunlin and a curlew feed on the mudflats.

Purple sandpipers roosting at high tide on some stone sea defenses. These birds favour rocky coastlines and are therefore quite scarce winter visitors to us.

The vibrations from the tightly packed, fast moving feet of brent geese seem to act like raindrops and cause earthworms to rise to the surface. Typically the opportunist gulls have learnt this and actively follow the brent flocks. The other geese feeding in slower moving, less dense flocks do not appear to have the same effect and fail to attract the attention of the gulls.

Snipe feeding actively during the twilight merging of dusk into moonlight.

At dusk vast skeins of pinkfeet leave their inland feeding areas and head to their nightime roosts on the coast.

Hares and a highly territorial red-legged partridge.